T0197526

Yippee, It's Ramadan!

by
Farjana Khan

AuthorHouse™
1663 Liberty Drive
Bloomington, IN 47403
www.authorhouse.com
Phone: 833-262-8899

This book is printed on acid-free paper.

ISBN: ISBN: 978-1-4490-1064-5 (sc) (sc)

Library of Congress Control Number: 2010913211

Print information available on the last page.

Published by AuthorHouse 03/31/2023

authorHOUSE°

Thanks to my family for all their
support- Faruque Khan, Anwara
Khan, Feruze Khan, Michael Khan,
Feruza Khan, and Aleena Ahmed.

My brother and I look for the
new moon.

2

My brother yells, "There it is. Ramadan Mubarak everybody!"

First our family prepares for a day of fasting.

4

We eat a meal when the world seems to be sleeping.

My father reminds us that Muslims fast from sunrise to sunset. They don't eat or drink anything during those hours. This teaches Muslims to be thankful for what they have and care for others that are less fortunate. Also, Muslims give thanks for the holy book, the Quran.

My mother adds that some people don't have
to fast at all. These include young children,
the elderly, and sick.

Throughout the day, children play games.
Monopoly is my favorite.

Then we read the Quran.

9

The sun finally sets. It's time for Iftar.

My relatives come from afar to share the meal.

We all eat dates and pray.

After prayer we continue to eat.

My aunts eat firni.

My uncles are er b-ra and lem-..ade.

At night we all go to the mosque. We hear that the last ten nights of Ramadan are important. During one of these nights, the first verses of the Quran were revealed.

Then, my family gives money to help others in need.

As the day slowly comes to an end, I reach for my calendar and cross off day one of Ramadan. There are only 29 more days to go!

We all go to bed and prepare for the next day. Yippee! It's Ramadan.

Author's Note

Ramadan is the 9th month in the Islamic calendar. Each month begins with the sighting of the new moon. Therefore, the Muslim year is about 11 days shorter than the solar year. Thus, the date for Ramadan changes every year.

Ramadan is the month of fasting. Muslims do not eat from sunrise to sunset. This teaches Muslims discipline, patience, and gratitude. Also, the holy Quran was first revealed to Prophet Mohammed (Peace Be Upon Him) during this time. Initially, Muslims wake up before dawn. They eat an early meal called Suhur. This provides them with the energy needed to fast for the day.

Throughout the day, many Muslims recite the Quran. At sunset, families break their fast with a meal called Iftar. First they eat a date. This is the same way Prophet Mohammed (PBUH) and his companions broke their fast. Then some families eat firni (rice pudding) and bora (fried lentils).

Later, Muslims go to the mosque to perform special prayers. These prayers are called Taraweeh. The last ten nights of Ramadan are crucial. During one of these nights the first verses of the Quran were revealed to the Prophet by angel Gabriel. Muslims also give Zakat- money to help others in need. Finally, Muslims celebrate the completion of the 30 days of fasting with another holiday called Eid-ul-Fitr. Please purchase my other story to learn more about Eid-ul-Fitr.

Printed in the United States
by Baker & Taylor Publisher Services